Grammar Success

Raising Writing Standards

Pie Corbett Rachel Roberts

OXFORD

OXFORD
UNIVERSITY PRESS

Great Clarendon Street, Oxford OX2 6DP

Oxford University Press is a department of the University of Oxford.
It furthers the University's objective of excellence in research,
scholarship, and education by publishing worldwide in

Oxford New York

Athens Auckland Bangkok Bogotá Buenos Aires Calcutta
Cape Town Chennai Dar es Salaam Delhi Florence Hong Kong
Istanbul Karachi Kuala Lumpur Madrid Melbourne Mexico City
Mumbai Nairobi Paris São Paulo Shanghai Singapore Taipei
Tokyo Toronto Warsaw

with associated companies in Berlin Ibadan

Oxford is a registered trade mark of Oxford University Press in the
UK and in certain other countries

ISBN 0 19 834286 1

Typeset and designed by Oxford Designers & Illustrators, Oxford

Printed in Hong Kong

Preface

Grammar Success is about teaching children how to use grammar to improve their writing. It provides materials, not only to deepen children's grammatical understanding, but also to refine their grammatical skills and to enable them to apply these to their own writing.

The course is built around the National Literacy Framework sentence level objectives. However, where there are gaps in the framework (for instance, the omission of nouns from Year 3) these have been addressed. Each unit is broken down into three sessions, based around the Pupils' Book, Teacher's Book and the Overhead Transparency Pack.

Session 1 uses an OHT to introduce the grammatical objective to the children. This part of the session should be lively, and interactive. Children then deepen their understanding of the particular grammatical feature through various independent activities. By the end of Session 1, pupils should be in a position to define their understanding of the objective.

Session 2 uses the Pupils' Book unit, plus photocopiable activities in the Teacher's Book. Pupils focus upon the grammatical feature in the context of wide-ranging stimulus texts. The children are asked comprehension questions on each text before moving into activities that focus upon the grammatical feature in use. By the end of this session, pupils have critically reflected upon the use of the objective through their reading.

Session 3 relates again to the text in the Pupils' Book, which now becomes a model for children's own writing. The teacher's notes describe in detail how to carry out shared writing, demonstrating how to use the grammatical feature in the process of writing a new text. A photocopiable Reminder Sheet in the Teacher's Book provides a summary, defining the grammatical feature and giving guidance on how to use it effectively in writing. It can be used for activities flagged by the symbol R. The session ends with pupils producing their own work, drawing on the shared writing experience.

While a full range of texts and outcomes are provided in the Pupils' Book, children will gain greater understanding of the grammar if all three elements of the course are available to them.

Activities are differentiated in both Pupils' Book (A–C) and Teacher's Book to allow for pupils who may struggle or who need an extra challenge. The photocopiable activities double as a valuable homework resource.

The course helps pupils to understand grammar but also to become skilful in the key grammatical skills of:

- Sentence construction
- Punctuation
- Enhancing writing with different language effects
- Cohesion – links with and between sentences, paragraphs and texts.

The more adept children are at using these skills in their writing, the more freedom they will have to focus upon the act of creative composition.

Pie Corbett

Sources

The texts used in this book are extracted from the following full sources, and we are grateful for their permission to reproduce copyright material.

p 8 From *The Wreck of the Zanzibar* by Michael Morpurgo (Heinemann, 1995), copyright © Michael Morpurgo 1995, reproduced by permission of the publishers, Wm Heinemann Ltd and Mammoth, an imprint of Egmont Children's Books Ltd.

p 10 'Wind Poem' by Pie Corbett, © Pie Corbett 1989, first published in John Foster (ed): *Another Fifth Poetry Book* (OUP, 1989), reproduced by permission of the author.

p 14 'Slowly' by James Reeves from *Complete Poems for Children* (Heinemann) reproduced by permission of Laura Cecil Literary Agency on behalf of the James Reeves Estate.

p 16 From *Climbing in the Dark* by Nick Warburton (Treetops Plays, OUP), reproduced by permission of Oxford University Press.

p 20 From *The Lion, the Witch and the Wardrobe* by C S Lewis, copyright © C S Lewis Pte. Ltd 1950 (Lions, 1980), reproduced by permission of The C S Lewis Company; from *Harry Potter and the Philosopher's Stone* by J K Rowling (Bloomsbury, 1997), reproduced by permission of the publishers.

p 22 'How Kites Fly', first published here, copyright © Pie Corbett 2000.

p 24 Lines from 'The Register' by Michael Rosen from *You Wait Till I'm Older than You* (Viking, 1996), © Michael Rosen 1996, reproduced by permission of PFD on behalf of Michael Rosen.

p 26 'The Pyramids', first published here, copyright © Pie Corbett 2000.

p 28 From *The Borrowers* by Mary Norton (J M Dent, 1958), © Mary Norton 1958, reproduced by permission of The Orion Publishing Group; from *Jet Smoke and Dragon Fire* by Charles Ashton (Walker Books Ltd, 1991), © Charles Ashton 1991, reproduced by permission of the publishers.

p 30 From *Harry Potter and the Philosopher's Stone* by J K Rowling (Bloomsbury, 1997), reproduced by permission of the publishers; from *The Soul Thieves* by Catherine Fisher (Bodley Head Children's Books, 1996), reproduced by permission of the Random House Group Ltd.

p 32 From 'Zaynab's Story' by Lawrence Crilley, written as part of a project at St Silas Church of England School, Liverpool, reproduced by permission of Liverpool Education and Lifelong Learning Service and the author.

p 34 'Brady's Story', first published here, copyright © Rachel Roberts 2000.

p 36 'Litterbugs', first published here, copyright © Rachel Roberts 2000.

p 38 Advertisement for Young Ornithologist's Club, reproduced by permission of the RSPB.

p 40 'You'd Better Beware' by Colin McNaughton from *There's an Awful Lot of Weirdos in our Neighbourhood* (Walker Books Ltd, 1987), text © Colin McNaughton 1987 and illustration © Colin McNaughton 1990, reproduced by permission of the publishers.

p 42 Adapted from 'Early Boats' in *The Book of Great Inventions* by Chris Oxlade, Steve Parker and Nigel Hawkes (Shooting Star Press), reproduced by permission of the publisher.

p 44 From *Little Burnt Face*, a retelling by K Locke and D Kennett (Keystone Picture Books), reproduced by permission of Era Publications.

Despite every effort to trace copyright holders, this has not been possible in every case. If notified, the publisher will be pleased to rectify any errors or omissions at the earliest opportunity

Contents

TERM 1

TERM 2

TERM 3

Checking your work

Here is the first draft of some instructions for having a good day out. The writer has not read it to check that all the verb tenses are correct or that the verbs agree grammatically. The order of the *What to do* list is also mixed up.

Recipe for a Great Day Out

I love holidays and having a day out. Does you? My ideal day out involves going to the beach. I liked plenty of lazing around, doing very little. I liking to read good books and laid around in the sun. However I did get boreded with this after a while because I also were enjoying swimming and playing games. So, I guessed I need a day out that are both lazy and active. What about you?

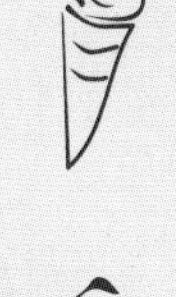

My ingredients:

You need a sunny day, a stretch of sand, a pile of good books, an ice-cream van, plenty of calm, blue water, several rock pools and sand dunes.

What to do:

A After a good read leave the family to simmer in a warm sea for an hour.

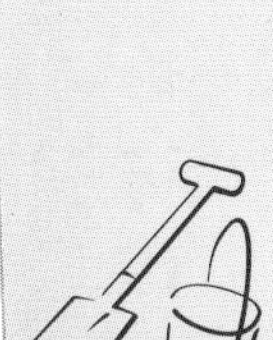

B Secondly, place a family where it is quiet, on golden, empty sand.

C Once dry, stir in an ice-cream van.

D In order to get dry, rub vigorously with big towels.

E As it is quiet, sprinkle on top several good books.

F At the end of the day, garnish with sand dunes till tired.

G First, take a sunny day.

Sounds pretty good to me. Why not invent your own recipe for a great day out, or a party?

Read through the recipe and discuss the following questions.

1 Think of three other ingredients for a good day at the beach.

2 What might be the purpose of writing like this about going to the beach?

3 What is the impact on the reader?

4 Why does the writer use questions in the recipe?

5 Rewrite the first paragraph making sure that the verbs agree and are in the correct tense.

6 Rearrange the *What to do* list A–G, so that it is in the correct order.

R

7 Take a piece of your work from a recent writing activity. Reread it and check it for errors. Correct these.

Once completed, swap your work with a partner's. See if you can find any mistakes that they may have missed. Check for:

- Agreement of verbs
- Consistency of tenses
- Good use of connectives to link sentences
- Well-ordered structure in the writing

UNIT 2 Verb tenses

And Now, the Weather

A

WEATHER OUTLOOK

Sunshine for a time tomorrow but the north and west will turn stormy by the evening with a risk of severe gales and heavy rain.

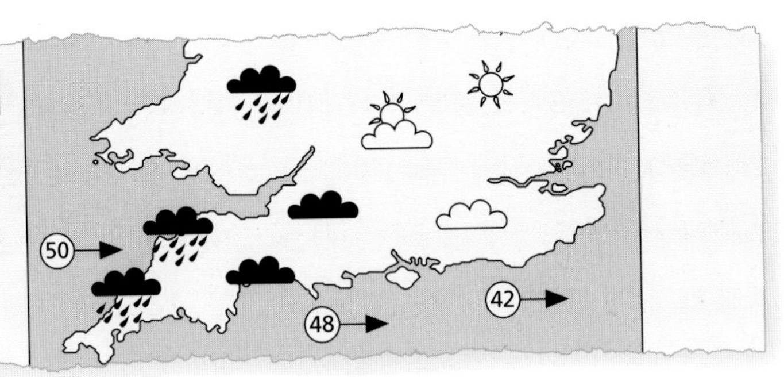

B

The storm was worse than ever. There must have been a dozen of us out doing the same thing on Great Porth, when someone saw the sail. The rain was coming in hail squalls, driving into my face so hard that I could scarcely open my eyes.

One sail became four, white against the black storm clouds. The ship was beating her way past Seal Rock towards the Tearing ledges, making no headway in the teeth of a gale. We all knew what was going to happen. We'd seen it before. A ship about to founder staggers before she falls. A huge wave broke over her stern and she did not come upright again. She lay on her side and wallowed in the waves.

The cry went up from all around. 'Wreck! Wreck!'

(From *The Wreck of the Zanzibar* by Michael Morpurgo)

C

LIGHTNING

Lightning is electricity that you can see. It is a sudden flow of electric current between two clouds, between a cloud and the ground, or between two parts of the cloud.

Read extracts A, B and C and discuss the following questions.

1 What types of text are extracts A, B and C?

2 Who might need to read them and why would they read them?

3 Who might have written them?

4 What types of text would you find them in?

5 Make a chart like the one below. Record in it the text type of each extract. Then make a note of which verb tense it is written in and explain why it is written in past, present or future.

	A	B	C
Text type Verb tense Why this tense?			

6 Choose one verb from each text and change its verb tense, for example: from past tense – to present – to future. A verb from extract B has been done for you.

One sail became four – One sail becomes four – One sail will become four…

7 What is the effect on your example of changing the verb tense?

8 Write three short weather reports: one for yesterday, one for today and a forecast for tomorrow. For each one you will need to decide on the appropriate tense to use. The editor has said that you can only have 25 words for each report.

When you finish, check the tense you have used in each report. Remember that you need to maintain the same tense throughout each one.

UNIT 3

Powerful verbs

Wind Poem

Wind slices its icy blade.

Wind raids trees,
Smacks leaves up back streets.

Wind somersaults sheets,
Bustles and kicks.

Wind flexes muscles,
Flicks its quivering wrist.

Wind twists dustbins
Into clattering cartwheels.

Wind curls its steel tongue
Like a shout flung at the sky.

Wind sighs;
Dies.

Pie Corbett

Read the poem and discuss the following questions.

1 What word best describes Wind's mood?
angry joyful energetic spiteful

2 Find and list as many words that rhyme (blade/raids) or almost rhyme (slices/icy). What effect do these rhymes have?

3 What is the effect of using short lines in the poem?

4 Collect and list all the powerful verbs. Why do you think the writer has used these verbs? Give your reasons like this.
I think he uses powerful verbs because....

5 The verbs make it sound as if Wind is alive.
Wind raids trees
Smacks leaves...

This is called personification. Write down three verbs from the poem that describe Wind's actions.

6 What is the effect of using verbs like this? Write down your ideas.
It makes it sound....

R

7 Write your own poem using powerful verbs to create an effect. Select verbs that personify to make it sound as if the subject is alive.

Choose an aspect of the weather such as rain, hail, snow, sleet or sun. Jot down words and phrases. Then try extending or trimming ideas to judge the effect.

Use a similar pattern to the *Wind Poem*. For example:
Sun sneaks
Round sleepy corners.

Sun peeks through windows,
Creeps into corners....

UNIT 4

Investigating adverbs

Four Endings

A

Wilbur never forgot Charlotte. Although he loved her children and grandchildren dearly, none of the new spiders ever quite took her place in his heart. She was in a class by herself. It is not often that someone comes along who is a true friend and a good writer. Charlotte was both.

(From *Charlotte's Web* by EB White)

B

'Night, Nanny,' he said, yawning.

Dimly he heard the goat reply, as she always did, 'Sleep tight. Mind the fleas don't bite,' and then, with a last couple of grunts, the Ace of Clubs drifted happily into dreamland.

(From *Ace* by Dick King-Smith)

C

The rain suddenly stopped and the sun warmed the back of my neck....

(From *The Butterfly Lion* by Michael Morpurgo)

D

Wearily the two boys trudged homewards. Tom stared at his friend. 'I'll run more carefully next time I'm near a cliff.'

(From *The Edge of Danger* by P Corbett)

1 Read extracts A, B, C and D and decide which ending matches each one from the list below:

- A character falling asleep happily is used to round off a story in a satisfying manner
- A change in weather is used to signal a happy ending
- The main character talks about what he has learned
- The main character remembers the key character

2 Write down one adverb with its verb from each extract, in a chart like the one below. Add a note about what the adverb is emphasizing. Extract A has been done for you.

Verb	Adverb	The adverb's job
loved	dearly	to show how fond Wilbur was of the baby spiders

3 Extract D starts with a sentence where the adverb is at the beginning. Rewrite the first sentence three times using different adverbs, and changing the verb to fit in. Beside each rewrite note down how the adverb alters the mood of the ending. For example:

Happily, the two boys ran homewards. – The boys are happy and want to get home quickly.

4 Create your own story ending. Select one of the types of ending from extracts A–D:

- Using weather to signal that this is the end
- Getting a character to comment on what has been learned
- Sending the main character into happy sleep
- Getting the main character to comment on another

Remember to select adverbs carefully, to add impact to the chosen ending. You may wish to include a sentence that starts with an adverb.

UNIT 5

Using adverbs

Slowly

Slowly the tide creeps up the sand,
Slowly the shadows cross the land.
Slowly the carthorse pulls his mile,
Slowly the old man mounts the stile.

Slowly the hands move round the clock,
Slowly the dew dries on the dock.
Slow is the snail – but slowest of all
The green moss spreads on the old brick wall.

James Reeves

Read the poem and discuss the following questions.

1 Which line makes the strongest picture in your mind?

2 What do these lines mean?
the carthorse pulls its mile
the old man mounts his stile
dew dries on the dock

3 How should the poem be read aloud?

4 List the verbs from the poem that go with the adverb *slowly*.
e.g. *slowly .... creeps* in the first line

5 Change the first five lines so that the adverb is *quickly*. Alter the verbs to match the adverb.
e.g. *Quickly the tide races up the sand*

6 Read the *slowly* and *quickly* versions of the poem aloud. How do they need to be read differently? Which sounds more effective?

7 The line *Slow is the snail* repeats the 's' sound. This special effect is called alliteration. Write down another example from the poem.

R

8 You are going to write an adverb poem using the same pattern as James Reeves' poem. Decide on an adverb, e.g. quickly, carefully, silently, calmly, stormily, quietly, smoothly, loudly, noisily, etc.

Brainstorm a list of things that act in this manner. Turn the list into simple poetic statements, making sure that you match the adverbs and the verbs. The verbs will probably be powerful verbs that describe actions precisely. For example:
Silently, the fog slips across town.
Silently, the cat pads through the grass...

Using a comma after the adverb will help to emphasize its meaning.

UNIT 6

Using commas

Climbing in the Dark

Will: My father sold me to Mr Fry, to go up chimbleys.

Tess: Sold you? Your own father?

Will: Yes. 'E took me to Fry's 'ouse one day and then went 'ome without me. I found meself in this cellar full of brushes and things. Then I knowed. I was sold, to go up chimbleys.

Tess: But that's terrible.

Will: That's fathers for you, miss. They're all the same.

Mrs Hutton: Whatever must it be like, climbing about in chimneys?

Will: It's 'orrible, miss. The bricks stay so 'ot it 'urts, and the chimbley's dark and it twists about so you don't know where you are. Mr Fry, 'e puts vinegar on me elbows and knees and stands me before the fire till I'm nearly roasted up.

Tess: But why does he do that?

Will: To 'arden the skin, miss. So I can grip on the chimbleys.

Mrs Hutton: Well, Will, there's some milk, and there's a spoon, and there's a pot of honey. You can help yourself to that.

Nick Warburton

Read the play extract through and discuss the following questions. Provide details from the text to support your ideas.

1 Who might Tess and Mrs Hutton be?

2 What does Tess feel about what has happened to Will?

3 What does Mrs Hutton think about this?

4 What do you think has happened just before this scene?

5 What do you think might happen next?

6 List all the examples of a comma being used to:

- Add a pause mid-sentence to help the reader
- Mark a character's name or title
- Separate items in a list

Write them down in a chart like this.

Adds a pause	Marks a name	In a list
Sold me to Mr Fry, to go...	That's fathers for you, miss	

7 Why is it particularly helpful to use commas in a playscript?

8 Why is Will's speech not always spelt correctly or spelt out in full?

R

9 Write a short extract from the next scene in the play. What will happen if Tess's father discovers Will – or Mr Fry bursts in to find Will?

Use commas to help the reader by separating parts of sentences, often when there are pauses in speech. Also remember to use commas for any sort of list and where a character's name or title is used.

You could start your scene like this.
(The door is flung open. A large man bursts in looking furious.)

UNIT 7 Editing and revising

Here is a draft report about what happened to evacuees during World War 2. The writer still needs to check the spelling and punctuation and to revise some of the sentences so that they are correct and easier to read.

The Evacuation

When World War 2 started many children was evacuated from the cities to the safety of the countryside and in the first three days of september 1939 nearly three million children was evacuated and most of them was labelled like luggage and separated from their parents and most of the children didn't know where they was going or if they will come back.

The childrens parents sent their children away and they was afriad of the german bombers It was a problem that there was not enough places for the children to go to. The children was just lined up against a wall and local people walked up and down picking out which ones they will take away.

Some children was lucky and were treated well and was like a proper member of the family that they end up with. Some people still remember their first go at living in the country and the kindly way that they was looked after and other children was beaten and cruelly.

let us hope that we never have to evacuate children again. Evacuation saved some lives, and for many children it was good and for many children it was a miserable time away from their families and they did not know if they were alive or dead.

Read through the text and discuss the following questions.

1 Why were children evacuated during the war?

2 What did the children think about the experience?

3 Name two problems with evacuation.

4 In paragraph one there are a number of key points, e.g. *first three days of September 1939; 3 million children evacuated.*

5 Pick out the writer's key points in paragraphs two and three. Write these in note form, e.g. *children labelled like luggage.*

6 Read paragraphs two, three and four. Rewrite them, revising for improvement and editing for accuracy.

Revising checklist

- Write in sentences and vary them to avoid rambling sentences.
- Use connecting words other than *and* and *then* to join sentences.
- Add in detail, using powerful verbs, adverbs and adjectives carefully.
- Structure the writing and make sure that sentences follow on from each other.

Editing checklist

- Correct spelling and punctuation.
- Make sure that verbs agree.

R

7 Choose one piece of your writing from this term. Read it and then revise and edit it. Copy out the revised text and present it neatly.

Use the list above to check that you have revised and edited all parts of the text.

Using adjectives

Creating Settings

A

On a windy hill, half hidden by trees and swirling mist, stood a stone cottage. A man hammered desperately on the door with his fists, calling a name and pleading for help.

(From *Sign of the Lion* by Sheryl Jordan)

B

They clung to each other on the roof, swaying drunkenly with the frost gleaming hard on the skylights. Above them, a crescent moon was etched against the swollen clouds that raced across the chill darkness of the night sky.

(From *Streetwise* by Anthony Masters)

C

Then Mr Tumnus stopped and took a flaming piece of wood out of the fire with a neat little pair of tongs, and lit a lamp. 'Now we shan't be long,' he said, and immediately put a kettle on.

Lucy thought she had never been in a nicer place. It was a little, dry, clean cave of reddish stone with a carpet on the floor and two little chairs ('one for me and one for a friend,' said Mr Tumnus) and a table and a dresser and a mantelpiece over the fire and above that a picture of an old Faun with a grey beard. ...There was a brown egg, lightly boiled, for each of them, and then sardines on toast, and then buttered toast, and then toast with honey, and then a sugar-coated cake.

(From *The Lion, the Witch and the Wardrobe* by CS Lewis)

D

Then they visited the Apothecary, which was fascinating enough to make up for its horrible smell, a mixture of bad eggs and rotted cabbages. Barrels of slimy stuff stood on the floor, jars of herbs, dried roots, and bright powders lined the walls, bundles of feathers, strings of fangs and snarled claws hung from the ceiling ...Harry himself examined silver Unicorn horns at twenty-one Galleons each and miniscule glittery-black beetle eyes (five Knuts a scoop).

(From *Harry Potter and the Philosopher's Stone* by JK Rowling)

Read the story extracts and discuss the following questions.

1 In extract A the first sentence describes the place. The second sentence introduces the character. Which words in these sentences establish the atmosphere?

2 Pick out three adjectives and their nouns that help to create the scene in extract B.

3 What sort of atmosphere is created in extract C? How does CS Lewis make it sound as if it would be rather nice to visit Mr Tumnus?

4 List nouns and their accompanying adjectives from extract D.

5 JK Rowling uses plenty of detail in extract D. How do you think Harry is feeling, and what might he be thinking? Support your answers with quotes from the extract.

6 Suggest suitable adjectives for any nouns in extract D that do not have one.

R

7 Use the structure of extract A as a basis for creating several different openings to stories or chapters.

In the first sentence, or first few sentences, describe the place and the weather, time of day/season. Then follow this with a sentence that introduces a character. Try to create an atmosphere by linking what the character is doing with the atmosphere created by the weather.

When you finish the first opening, try writing another, choosing a completely different setting, weather and main character.

UNIT 9 Different adjectives

How Kites Fly

Kites are a form of airborne craft that are heavier than air but are not powered by anything other than the wind itself.

Kites can be made of lightest materials such as paper, nylon or cotton as long as they are strong. Kites come in various shapes and sizes – from the smallest pocket kites to the largest display kites. They are usually flown from the ground and are easiest to fly from the highest hilltops because they need quite a strong breeze of about 12–30 kilometres per hour to stay up. If the wind is not strong enough, they will not fly. The breeze pushes underneath the kite, causing it to lift upwards. To keep the kite at its steadiest in the air, and stop it dipping and diving, you have to attach the sleekest tail. It can also be useful to have more than one control line to help maintain the kite's stable flight.

The Chinese are the world's greatest kite flyers – they have flown kites since 1000 BC – but it was not until the Thirteenth Century that kites were introduced by traders into Europe. At one time they were used to frighten off evil spirits from houses. For this reason they were flown late in the darkest night from rooftops. Since then kites have been used by the army, for signalling, for fishing and as a sport.

Kite flying can be a fun-filled hobby. Try it. Feel the breeze uplift the swiftest kite to great heights – and feel your spirit fly too!

Read the text and discuss the following questions.

1 Who would have written a text like this – and what did they need to know before they began writing?

2 Where might you read this text?

3 Identify the sentence where the writer explains how a kite actually gets up into the air.

4 In the sentence you have identified, which is the key word?

5 Find all the examples of superlative adjectives being used in paragraph two. Complete a chart like this one:

Adjective	Comparative	Superlative
light	lighter	lightest

R

6 Take a subject that you know about, such as *How to keep warm*, *How to separate solids from liquids* or *How friction works*. Write an explanatory text.

Use the following structure as a guide, and select any adjectives carefully.

Para 1: Introduction
Para 2: Explanation of the subject
Para 3: Further interesting facts
Para 4: Concluding points for reader to remember

UNIT 10 Using apostrophes

The Register

Right Class 6
Register time –
That means everyone sitting down.
Everyone, Darren.
No, Darren, we're not feeding the snails now.
Sarah, could you pass me the register?
No I haven't got it, you've got it.
You went to fetch it, remember?
Oh that was yesterday, was it?
Darren, leave the snails alone.
One moment everyone, Mr Hardware wants a word.
Right Class 6
Mr Hardware says that any tennis balls landing
In the gutter by the kitchen will be left there till
Christmas
When they'll be sent to Dr Barnardo's.
No, he's not my doctor, Louise,
My doctor doesn't need tennis balls.
Dr Barnardo's not alive he's –
I know, Wayne, that if he's not alive
He can't use the tennis balls.
Darren, don't touch the snails, do you hear me?
Does anyone know who or what is Dr Barnardo's?
No, Hugh, not a dogs' home.
Yes, Abdul, a children's home, well done…

Michael Rosen

Read through the poem and discuss the following questions. Provide details from the text to support your ideas.

1 Who is Mr Hardware?

2 How does the teacher feel about Darren?

3 What do you think the children think of their teacher?

4 What kinds of things does your teacher always say at register time?

5 List all the words from the poem that use an apostrophe for omission. Then write down what the full version should be, as shown in this example.

Word with apostrophe	Complete phrase
don't	do not

6 List all the words that use an apostrophe to show possession. Note down their meanings, as shown in the example below.

Phrase with apostrophe	What it means
Dr Barnardo's	The home belonging to Dr Barnardo

7 How does using apostrophes help the teacher's words sound more like speech?

R

8 Use the poem to write the next part of the teacher's monologue as she takes the register.

Try to use particular expressions that teachers use. As you are writing a piece of speech, you may use apostrophes to show omission in words such as *don't, can't,* etc.

The challenge is also to weave into the speech the use of an apostrophe for possession. For instance, you could mention *Darren's bag,* or *Wayne's pencil.*

UNIT 11 Exploring word order

ENCYCLOPEDIA DELUXE EDITION

▼ Feature ▼ Options ▼ ® ◀ ▶ Find Home Dictionary Research Organizer

THE PYRAMIDS

More Information about this subject

Pyramids at Giza

Expand Caption

Pyramids were built as enormous tombs for the Egyptian royalty – the pharaohs. The Egyptians believed that the pharaohs were gods in the shape of men and worshipped them. They brought huge blocks of stone by boat along the River Nile to the site of the pyramids. They took years to build each tomb, constructing them with gangs of slaves who moved the massive blocks of stone into place on sledges. There were no cranes to help them.

BUILDING THE PYRAMIDS

The pyramids are found on the west bank of the River Nile in Northern Africa. They are massive four-sided buildings, with a square base and triangular sides that meet at the top in a point.

The Egyptians built the pyramids between 2700 BC and 1000 BC. The first was built in about 2650 BC at Sakkara. The pyramids at Giza, near Cairo, are the only one of the original Seven Wonders of the World that is left standing.

THE PYRAMIDS TODAY

There are about 80 pyramids still standing. They are covered with hieroglyphics, which is an early form of writing that uses pictures instead of an alphabet. Many people nowadays like to take a cruise down the River Nile and visit the ancient tombs. The pyramids act as a reminder that many past civilizations could build great wonders without today's technology.

Read the text about the pyramids and discuss the following questions.

1 Where are the pyramids found?

2 Who built them (make two points in your answer)?

3 Why were they built (make two points in your answer)?

4 Give two reasons why people visit the pyramids nowadays.

5 Reread paragraphs three and four.

Turn them into a list of key points – using note-form and not full sentences.

You may need to use headings to help you organize the information, like this:

Paragraph 3 What the pyramids were used for:
– tombs for pharaohs – Egyptian royalty
– worshipped as gods by Egyptian people

R

6 Rewrite the text using your notes to create a simple account of the pyramids, aimed at children aged 7 years old.

The text should be clear and to the point. It must not be too difficult. Only use the key pieces of information and particular details that you believe would interest your audience.

UNIT 12 *Joining & separating clauses*

Creating Imaginary Worlds

A

The floor of the sitting-room was carpeted with deep red blotting-paper, which was warm and cosy, and soaked up the spills. Homily would renew it at intervals when it became available upstairs, but since Aunt Sophy had taken to her bed, Mrs Driver seldom thought of blotting-paper unless, suddenly, there were guests. Homily liked things which saved washing because drying was difficult under the floor; water they had in plenty, hot and cold, thanks to Pod's father who had tapped the pipes from the kitchen boiler.

(From *The Borrowers* by Mary Norton)

B

He found the old man without difficulty, but there was little comfort to be had from him. It seemed the dragon was secure for the time being. 'I've got him here somewhere,' he said, and bent down and rummaged about in the drawer behind the chair. When he stood again, he had a bottle in his hand. It was an ordinary clear glass bottle with a cork in the top, and a heavy green seal keeping the cork in. Sparrow could hardly believe his eyes: inside the bottle was the dragon.

It looked extremely cross, and when Puckel lifted the bottle for Sparrow to see it, it spouted smoke and tiny red flames at them. The smoke drifted up and gathered in a black clot in the neck of the bottle. At the bottom was a little rough pyramid of rock.

'I shrank him,' Puckel explained, 'but a stupid mountain went and got in the way...'

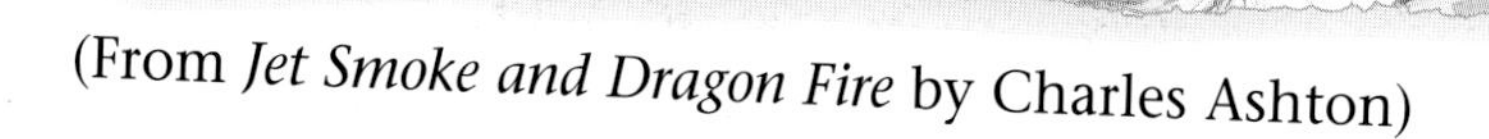

(From *Jet Smoke and Dragon Fire* by Charles Ashton)

Read extracts A and B and discuss the following questions.

1 In extract A, why is the blotting-paper in the sitting-room so useful?

2 How do the family manage to have hot and cold water?

3 In extract B, find two things that you know about Puckel, quoting from the text.

4 Find three details that the writer gives about the bottle.

5 How does Puckel know the dragon is cross?

6 Why do you think the narrator suggests that the dragon was only secure for the time being?

7 Identify the two clauses in the first sentence of extract B. Write down and underline each clause in a different colour. Then, circle the linking device used. Is it a comma or a conjunction?

8 Find another sentence with two clauses from either extract. Underline and circle this in the same way. Rewrite it as if it were two sentences. Read it again and decide which sentence sounds more fluent and why.

R

9 Continue the story about the dragon in the bottle. Write the next few paragraphs. Concentrate upon how you join clauses, varying the opening of your sentences and sentence length. Use some short sentences for dramatic effect. Try a range of conjunctions to help link clauses, e.g. after, although, and, as, as if, as long as, as though, because, before, but, if, in case, once, or, since, than, that, though, till, until, unless, when, whenever, where, wherever, whereas, while.

You could begin like this:

At that moment Puckel slipped. It could have happened to anybody but it was the worst possible thing that could happen. The glass jar shattered...

UNIT 13

Dramatic sentences

Three Exciting Moments

A

Harry had never even imagined such a strange and splendid place. It was lit by thousands and thousands of candles which were floating in mid-air over four long tables, where the rest of the students were sitting. These tables were laid with glittering golden plates and goblets. At the top of the hall was another long table where the teachers were sitting. Professor McGonagall led the first years up here, so that they came to a halt in a line facing the other students, with the teachers behind them. The hundreds of faces staring at them looked like pale lanterns in the flickering candlelight. Dotted here and there among the students, the ghosts shone misty silver. Mainly to avoid all the staring eyes, Harry looked upwards and saw a velvety black ceiling dotted with stars. He heard Hermione whisper, 'It's bewitched to look like the sky outside, I read about it in *Hogwarts, a History.*'

(From *Harry Potter and the Philosopher's Stone* by JK Rowling)

B

She was at him like a cat, so fast that she seemed a blur, and yet his mind took it all in.

I hit her. The arrow hit her in the neck. She's charging. She's charging at me. Another arrow. No, no time. The lance. That's it, the lance.

(From *Hatchet Winter* by Gary Paulsen)

C

Skapti hauled her up.

'What is it?' she gasped.

'Keep quiet!'

Silent, they waited, letting the long echoes fade. The walls quivered once, and were still.

'An earthquake?' Skapti breathed.

Something crashed out in the hall, settling to stillness.

'Could be.' Brochael stood tense. 'If so we should get outside. There'll be others.'

'It could have been something else,' Jessa muttered.

'A giant walking?' Skapti suggested.

They were silent, despite the scorn in his tone....

(From *The Soul Thieves* by Catherine Fisher)

Read extracts A, B and C and discuss the following questions.

1 In extract A, how do you think Harry and Hermione feel about what they are watching?

2 Why do you think Harry looks upwards?

3 Choose three dramatic details from the description of the dining hall.

4 The hero in extract B is being attacked by a moose. How does the writer make this sound exciting?

5 What does it mean in extract C, when the writer says that Skapti speaks with scorn in his voice?

6 List three ways in which extract A differs from extracts B and C.

7 List examples of the different techniques used in extracts B and C to create suspense. Think about each writer's use of:

- Questions
- Short sentences
- Powerful verbs
- Personification
- Alliteration
- Details giving hints about hidden dangers

8 Rewrite extract C using conjunctions to join the sentences, and make them more elaborate. Does this make the passage more or less exciting?

R

9 Continue extract C. Use a range of techniques to gain effects. Use short sentences for dramatic effect, and longer ones for description. Try out other techniques such as alliteration, similes, powerful verbs, personification and questions. You could begin:

Skapti turned to Jessa. He pressed an urgent finger to his lips. 'Shhh,' he hissed.

They made their way down the stone steps towards the cellars. In the distance they could hear the sound of breathing, a heavy rasping voice in the darkness muttering...

Punctuation in sentences

ZAYNAB'S STORY

On the yard at lunchtime there was a general air of excitement: girls stood chatting and skipping; boys played football. Zaynab found a quiet corner and tried to stay out of the way.

'Zaynab, Zaynab!' Alison was standing with Kealey and Halima on the far side of the yard, waving to her. Zaynab smiled, waved back, and made her way over to join them.

As she made her way across to her friends, Zaynab was knocked to the ground. At first she thought it was an accident, but she knew from the shrieks of laughter and the taunts from the boys that it had been deliberate, and that Tony was to blame. If she hadn't been crying from the pain in her leg, she would have cried tears of embarrassment.

'Now look what you've done!' shouted Alison from across the yard.

Zaynab leapt to her feet and ran. She ran straight past the door monitors, and didn't even stop when she heard the dinner ladies calling her back. She carried on running until she reached the girls' toilets.

Slamming the door behind her, Zaynab slumped to the floor and sobbed. What could she do?

'Alison, what has happened to Zaynab?' asked Mrs Taylor. Alison told Mrs Taylor how Zaynab had been bullied by Tony and his friends, and how they had tripped her up on the school yard. Alison told Mrs Taylor that Zaynab had run into the toilets.

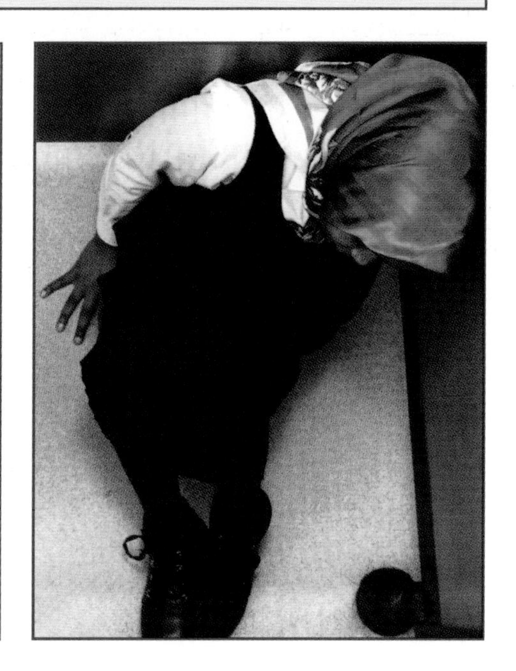

'Zaynab, Zaynab, are you all right, dear?' Mrs Taylor called. Inside, Zaynab sat on the floor in tears. Eventually the door opened slowly, and a tearful-looking Zaynab stood sniffing before Mrs Taylor. Mrs Taylor handed her a tissue.

Lawrence Crilley

Read the story through and discuss the following questions.

1 Suggest why Zaynab looks for somewhere quiet to stand in the yard.

2 How do you think Zaynab feels when Alison calls to her?

3 Why do you think Tony trips Zaynab?

4 How do you think Mrs Taylor will help Zaynab?

5 Find and copy out a sentence which contains:

- A comma
- A colon
- A semi-colon
- Speech marks

Highlight the punctuation mark in each sentence.

6 Here are some sentences from the extract. After each one there is a list. Try to write a sentence like each one from the extract, using items from the list.

On the yard at lunchtime there was a general air of excitement: girls stood chatting and skipping; boys played football.

park   Saturday   children cycling   toddlers swinging

If she hadn't been crying from the pain in her leg, she would have cried tears of embarrassment.

laughing at clown   laughed at Mum

Slamming the door behind her, Zaynab slumped to the floor and sobbed.

opening door   walked in   shouted

R

7 In *Zaynab's Story*, a girl is being bullied. She becomes very upset, until one of her classmates helps her by telling an adult. Use this simple structure to write a story of your own about bullying.

Remember to punctuate your writing carefully, so that its meaning is crystal clear.

UNIT 15

Connectives in sentences

Brady's Story

I feel like I've been here for days, but it's probably only a couple of hours. Dad came to pick me up from school when Mrs Robinson called, and he sent me straight up to my room.

Bullying, they told her. Me – bullying Shane Gulliver. I wouldn't do that. I don't like the kid, but I wouldn't bully him – I wouldn't bully anyone. Still, I'm here in my room on my own, so someone thinks I did.

This morning, I went to school and, as usual, Shane started. He can be a *real* pain. I tried to ignore him, but after he called me 'gingernut' for the sixth time, I pushed him. I know I shouldn't have, but what would *you* have done?

On the one hand, it's just not right to hit people. Dad is always telling me that it doesn't solve any problems. On the other hand, I couldn't let him get away with it. Everyone would have thought I was soft.

Dad has told me I have to apologise – in front of the whole class! I've got to decide what to do.

If I do apologise, Shane is going to think he's won. David and Chris will have a good laugh, too. They'll take the mickey out of me for weeks.

If I don't apologise, though, I'll never be allowed out again. My dad is really upset, and I hate it when he's upset with me. Mrs Robinson says she's disappointed, too.

So, on balance, I think I'll just go ahead and apologise. I'll do it tomorrow, first thing. If David and Chris laugh at me, who cares? They wouldn't have the guts to apologise. Dad says it takes real courage to admit you were wrong.

Shane Gulliver had better be careful, though…

Read Brady's story through and discuss the following questions.

1 How do you think Brady was feeling when he pushed Shane?

2 What could Brady have done, instead of pushing Shane?

3 What is the main reason Brady does not want to apologise to Shane? Explain your answer.

4 Brady will probably feel a lot of different emotions when he apologises to Shane. List at least three emotions that you think he might feel.

5 Copy out three sentences from the story which contain connecting words and phrases. Underline the connecting words and phrases.

6 Rewrite some of these sentences using different connecting words and phrases. Decide which is the best version of the sentence and identify it with a tick.

7 Write a script for Brady's apology. This should be between 20 and 30 words. Try to include at least two sentences that use connecting words and phrases.

R

8 Write a journal entry for Shane. Do you think he will have been punished, too? Put his side of the story, and explain the problem which faces him.

Remember to use a range of connecting words and phrases, like the ones used in Brady's story.

UNIT 16

Structure & connectives

LITTERBUGS

Last week my Dad went abroad on a business trip. When he came home, he was horrified by the amount of litter blowing around the streets, on railway lines and in shopping centres. He saw hardly any litter while he was away, and he had not realized before how horrible it is here.

Many beautiful towns and cities are ruined by people who are lazy and selfish: people who leave litter behind them. People who drop litter are disgusting, and they should be punished.

First of all, litter is ugly. It can make the loveliest place seem untidy and uncared for, so that visitors do not want to return.

Secondly, litter is unhealthy. It can attract rats and other pests, which carry disease, so that people may fall ill. Rats are also dangerous because they can bite.

Finally, litter is wasteful. Many items that are thrown away are actually recyclable. If people recycled drink cans, instead of throwing them on the ground or behind hedges and walls, the Earth's resources would be preserved.

It does not take long to put a crisp packet or sweet wrapper into a litterbin, yet litterbugs simply don't bother. Their lack of thought puts people's livelihoods and even lives at risk. This is why it is important to impose heavy fines on litterbugs: only by doing this can we make them realize how serious a crime littering really is. Everyone should make it their business to make sure that no one drops litter while they are around. In this way we will make our towns and cities beautiful again, and they will be safer places for everyone.

What part will you play?

Read the text through and discuss the following questions.

1 Give three main reasons why the writer thinks litter is bad.

2 Decide which reason is the most important to you, and explain why.

3 How would you stop people dropping litter?

4 What would you say to a friend who dropped a crisp packet in the playground?

5 Why do you think the writer has finished the piece with a question?

6 Adverbs sometimes end in *-ly*. Make a list of all the words in this passage that end in *-ly*; underline the ones which are adverbs.

7 In pieces of argument, writers often use sentences beginning with *If...* to persuade people. Find a sentence beginning with *If* in this piece.

Write two more sentences beginning with *If* to explain why life would be better without litter.

R

8 The writer of this piece has tried to persuade the reader to make sure that they do not drop litter. She does this by:

- Explaining what the problem is
- Giving three reasons for people to change their behaviour
- Saying what could be done to make them change

Use this plan to help you write an argument to persuade people to improve the environment in your school.

Different sentence types

LOOK WHAT YOU GET

when you join the YOC, the world's biggest wildlife club for young people.

YOC MEMBERSHIP PACK

Discover a new world of wildlife with the YOC

Find out about all sorts of amazing birds and wildlife.

JOIN NOW, AND YOU GET

- a Get Wild book crammed with facts, figures, puzzles and pictures
- a great colourful magazine six times a year, a stunning poster of a barn owl and your own YOC membership card
- free entry to 120 nature reserves

PLUS A FREE

Wildfile magnetic pocket organizer with a diary, factfile and jokes pages.

MEMBERSHIP FORM ONE child £10 ☐ *OR* for ALL children at the same address £14 ☐

Name ______ Date of birth* ______

Name ______ Date of birth* ______

Name ______ Date of birth* ______

Address ______

______ Postcode ______

I enclose a cheque/PO payable to YOC ☐ or debit my Mastercard /Visa card no ______ Expiry date ______

Cardholder's name ______

Signature ______

Address *(if different from above)* ______

**You don't have to give us your date of birth, but doing so lets us send you the correct information for your age group and enter you into a birthday draw*

RSPB The YOC is the junior membership of The Royal Society for the Protection of Birds.

(From RSPB advertisement in *Art Attack* magazine)

Read the advertisement and discuss the following questions.

1 Name three things you would get if you join the YOC.

2 Some of the advertisement is written in capital letters. Explain why.

3 Do you think this club is good value? Give three reasons for your answer.

4 This advertisement comes from a children's magazine. Suggest three other places the YOC could advertise.

5 In the advertisement, find one example of a statement and one of an instruction.

Then change one of these sentences into a question, and the other into an exclamation.

6 Write a short explanation of how you changed one sentence into another. You should write about:
- How you changed the word order
- The words you added in or took out
- Any changes you made to punctuation

R

7 Magazines often have advertisements for clubs. Write an advert for a club to which you already belong, or which you would like to start up. You could use a structure like the YOC advertisement:
- Use a headline to grab attention
- Explain what the club is
- Explain what you get if you join
- Write a membership form

Remember to use different sentence types. Try to include statements, instructions and at least one question.

UNIT 18

Suffixes

YOU'D BETTER BEWARE

You'd better beware, if you come round here,
To watch your step, to steer well clear
Of my front gate, it's a dangerous place
Because you might come face to face
With my new pet who's big and mean,
The ugliest brute you've ever seen.

Crooks and robbers don't come near,
They creep right past, they shake with fear,
They'd rather spend a year in gaol
Than risk one tickle from his fingernail.
Claws like razors, teeth like knives,
They'd better get lost, better run for their lives.

So if you're broke or out of work,
Get pushed around and called a jerk,
And if you're sad or if you're blue,
Take my advice, this is what you do:
Go down to the monster store
And get yourself a dinosaur.

Beat that drum, bang that gong,
Six metres high by sixteen long,
Come on all and join the chorus:
My new pet's a Tyrannosaurus!

Colin McNaughton

Read the poem through and discuss the following questions:

1 Give three advantages of having a pet dinosaur.

2 Give three disadvantages of having a pet dinosaur.

3 How would you persuade your family to buy a dinosaur from the monster store?

4 Why is this poem called *You'd Better Beware*? Give two reasons.

5 Find two lines in the poem which have ten syllables. Copy these out.

6 Look at the highlighted words in this table. Decide what type of word each one is. Change the ending to make it into a different word type.

Sentence	Type of word	New word type	New sentence
...it's a *dangerous* place	adjective	noun	There is great *danger.*
Crooks and robbers don't come near		adjective	
Crooks and *robbers* don't come near		verb	
Go down to the *monster* store...		adjective	
Beat that *drum* ...		verb	

R

7 The poem is a rap about a pet dinosaur. Try writing a rap about a friend with magic powers. Use the same pattern of rhythm and rhyme as the dinosaur poem. The first two lines have been written for you.

You'll be amazed if you come to our school,
I've got a friend who can break every rule...

Remember to check the spelling of word endings.

UNIT 19

Changing sentence types

EARLY BOATS

The first 'boats' were probably logs, bundles of reeds or inflated animal skins, bound together to form rafts. The first true boat was probably a hollowed-out log. The discovery that such objects could float in water was made in many parts of the world. Many of these first boats are still used around the world today.

EGYPTIAN RAFTS were made from bundles of papyrus tied together. They were used on the River Nile from about 7,000 BC. In 1970 a Norwegian, called Thor Heyerdaal, sailed Ra II, a boat made from papyrus reeds, across the Atlantic from Africa to the West Indies.

DUGOUT CANOES were one of the earliest forms of simple boat. Hollowed out from a tree trunk, they were shaped to give increased speed. The outrigger canoes of the Pacific islands are still based on the dugout principles.

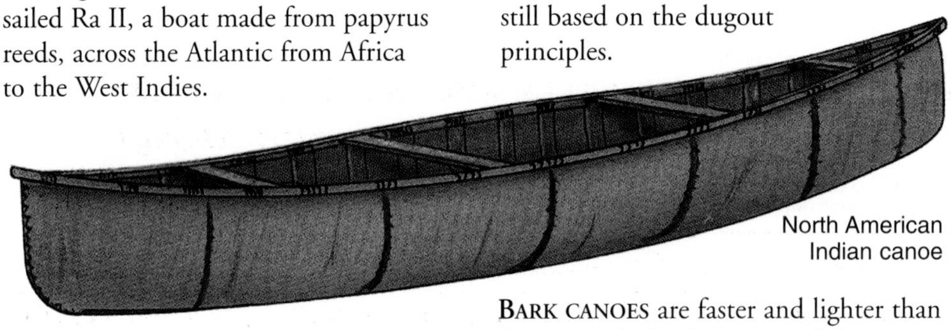

North American Indian canoe

BARK CANOES are faster and lighter than dugouts. The bark is stripped from a large tree in one piece and stretched over a wooden framework. Bark canoes were made extensively by the North American Indians and are still made by the Aborigines of Australia.

CORACLES are still used for fishing on certain rivers in Wales today. Originally, a thin frame was covered by animal skins, but this has been replaced by tar-covered canvas today. Quffa basket boats are used on the Rivers Tigris and Euphrates in Iraq. Unlike the coracle, they can hold twenty people.

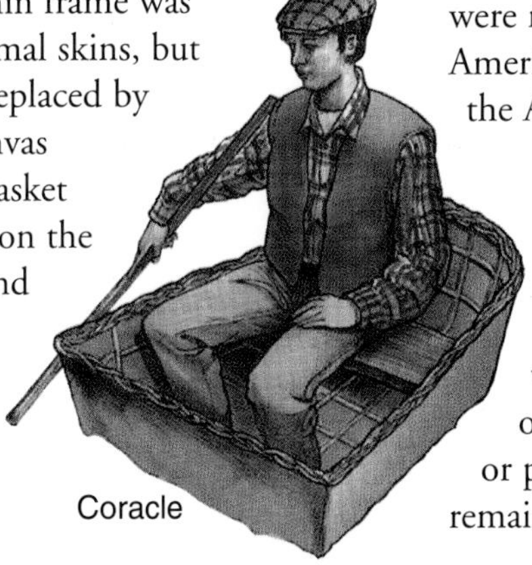

Coracle

The past today

The coracle, quffa and bark canoe are still used. Today's modern windsurfers and kayaks are made of modern materials like fibreglass or plastic, but their shape and design remain similar to the original craft.

Adapted from *The Book of Great Inventions* by Chris Oxlade, Steve Parker and Nigel Hawkes

Read the text through and discuss the following.

1 List four types of early boats.

2 Copy and complete a table like the one below, using information from the text.

Name	Country	Material	Still used?

3 Why do you think people tried to build boats? Give three reasons.

4 What do you think it was like in Thor Heyerdaal's boat?

5 The sentences on the left below are statements. Make each into a different sort of sentence by changing the word order, adding or deleting words or changing the punctuation. The first has been done.

Sentence	Question	Exclamation	Instruction
Bark canoes are faster and lighter than dugouts.	Are bark canoes faster than dugouts?	Bark canoes are far faster than dugouts!	You should make bark canoes faster and lighter than dugouts.
Hollowed out from a tree, dugouts were shaped to give more speed.			
Quffa basket boats are used on the Rivers Tigris and Euphrates.			
The coracle, quffa and bark canoe are still used.			

6 Use the information you have written in your version of the chart above to write an article about early boats. Try using some different sorts of sentences to make the text more interesting.

UNIT 20 Word endings & word classes

Little Burnt Face

There once lived a great warrior who had three daughters. His wife had been long dead, and it was left to the two older daughters to care for their younger sister.

The third daughter was very beautiful. She was much loved by all who knew her, but her sisters were harsh with her, for they were filled with jealousy. When their father was away they clothed her in rags and made sure that she had the dirtiest jobs to do. When he was around they were a little less cruel, but they always made their harshness appear to be for the child's own good.

It was her duty always to clean the place where the fires were made and to collect materials to keep the fire going. So the older sisters cut her long black hair on the pretext that it might fall into the fire and burn. They then made her work close to the fire so that sparks would mark her face and she would no longer be beautiful.

When her father asked how her face had become so scarred, they spoke scornfully of a clumsy child who was disobedient, fell into the fire and had to be rescued by her older sisters. So her father scolded her for her naughtiness and she was unhappy, for she loved her father dearly.

In this way the years went by, Little Burnt Face growing even more beautiful in spite of the cruel treatment shown by her sisters. Everybody loved her even though her sisters told dreadful tales about her 'wilfulness and disobedience' towards them.

(Adapted from a retelling by *K Locke and D Kennett*)

Read the story through and discuss the following questions.

1 Does this story remind you of any others? Name one and explain the similarities.

2 How do you think Little Burnt Face might feel about her sisters?

3 How do you think the two sisters feel about the younger one?

4 Why does no one tell the father about the older sisters' behaviour?

5 What advice would you give to Little Burnt Face?

6 What sort of story is this? Give reasons to support your view.

7 Some words have endings that can be changed; this often helps us to work out what sorts of word they are. Create a table like this. Then write in each word in the second column, but without an ending, and decide what sort of word each is. The first has been done for you:

Word	Without ending	Word class
scolded	scold	verb
sparks		
older		
filled		
years		
going		

R

8 There are many traditional stories about sisters. In this Native American story, a great Chief called Strong Wind the Invisible decides to take a wife. He can only be seen by his sister, and he says that he will marry the first maiden who can see him clearly. How will he meet Little Burnt Face and what will happen next? Continue the story.

Plan your story in paragraphs, and check the spelling of word endings.

Glossary

adjective An adjective is a word that describes somebody or something.
1 Adjectives are usually found in front of a noun.
For example: *green* emeralds and *glittering* diamonds
2 In some cases, adjectives can come after a verb.
For example: It was *big*.
3 Sometimes you can use two adjectives together, e.g. *tall and handsome*. This is called an **adjectival phrase**.
4 Adjectives can be used to describe degrees of intensity. To make a **comparative** adjective you usually add *er* (or use *more*).
For example: *quick/quicker* *more beautiful*
5 To make a **superlative** you add *est* (or use *most*).
For example: *quickest* *most beautiful*

adverb An adverb adds further meaning to a verb. Many are formed by adding *ly* to an adjective, e.g. *slow/slowly*. They often come next to the verb in a sentence. Adverbs can tell the reader:
How: *quickly, stupidly, amazingly.* Where: *there, here, everywhere.*
When: *yesterday, today, now.* How often: *occasionally, often.*

agreement Agreement is the link between the subject of a sentence and the verb.
For example: *I am/I was* *You are/you were*
The storm was becoming worse *The storms were becoming worse*

apostrophe An apostrophe (') is a punctuation mark that is used in two ways.
1 To show where letters are missing, e.g. *don't, can't, I'm.*
2 To show possession, e.g. *my dog's collar*. This explains that the collar belongs to my dog. In the plural the apostrophe follows the *s*, e.g. *the boys' cards*. This explains that the cards belonged to the boys.
There is one exception. *Its* is used for possession and *It's* stands for *it is*.

bold Letters or words can be written in bold print, which is darker than normal. It can help to highlight words for the reader.
For example: *'Promise me, you will **never** do that again.'*

capital letter A capital letter starts the first word of a new sentence. It is a letter written in the upper case, e.g. JOIN NOW AND YOU GET.

caption A caption is a short sentence or phrase used with a picture.
For example: *Pyramids at Giza*

classic poetry This is poetry that has survived the test of time.

clause A clause is a group of words that shows an event. It contains a subject and a verb, e.g. *I ran*. In this clause, *I* is the subject and *ran* is the verb.

colon/ semi-colon A colon is a punctuation mark (:) often used either:
1 To introduce a list in instructions, e.g. *You will need: two tyres ...*
2 To add further information to a sentence, e.g. *I am quick at running: as fast as a cheetah.*
A semi-colon is a punctuation mark (;) that separates two main clauses, e.g. *I like cheese; it is delicious.*

commas A comma is a punctuation mark (,) used to separate parts in a sentence. When reading you have to leave a pause when there is a comma. Commas can be used:
1 To separate items in a list, e.g. *a sunny day, a stretch of sand, a pile of good books, several rock pools and an ice-cream van.*
2 To separate pieces of information, e.g. *That's true, yes, that's true.*
3 When addressing someone by name, e.g. *I know, Wayne.*

comparative See **adjective**.

conjunction A conjunction is a word used to link clauses within a sentence, e.g. *and, but, so, until, when, as*, e.g. *When he stood up, he had a book in his hand.*

connective A connective is a word or a phrase that links clauses or sentences. Connectives can be **conjunctions** (e.g. *but, when, because*) or connecting adverbs (e.g. *however, then, therefore*).

dash A dash is a punctuation mark (–) often used in informal writing or in place of other punctuation marks, e.g. *It was fun – we all loved it.*

definition A definition is an explanation of the meaning of a word.
For example: **purse** a small bag for holding money.

dialogue Dialogue is the term used to describe a conversation (See page 30.)

discussion writing This type of text sets out both sides of an argument and draws a conclusion, supported by reasoning and evidence. Discussion texts set out to provide a balanced argument. (See page 36.)

exclamation mark An exclamation mark is a punctuation mark (!) used to end an exclamation, such as joy, anger, surprise, e.g. *Oh dear!*

explanation This type of text explains a process: how or why things happen, e.g. *How a kite flies*. Explanations hinge around the word *because* as they are based on an explanation of 'cause' and 'effect'. (See page 22.)

full stop A full stop (.) is a punctuation mark used at the end of a sentence.
For example: *Wilbur never forgot Charlotte.*

heading A heading is a title that may be used to show the reader what a paragraph or section of text is about, e.g. *Early Boats*

hyphen A hyphen is a short dash used to join words together, e.g. *co-operate*.

instruction This text helps readers to make or learn something. (See page 6.)

italic Italic writing is a handwriting style that slopes. It can be used to help highlight words for the reader, e.g. (*Charlotte's Web* by E.B. White)

noun A noun is a word that names something or somebody.
For example: *fox, chicken, brother, rock, sea, cloud, picture.*

performance poetry This is a form of poetry that can be performed aloud, often with music or a number of readers. (See page 40.)

person (1st, 2nd, or 3rd person) 1st person is used to talk about oneself – *I/we*. 2nd person is used to talk about whoever is listening or reading – *you*. 3rd person is used to refer to someone or somebody else – *he, she, it, they*.
For example: *I* feel like *I*'ve been here for days.
Look what *you* get, when *you* join the YOC.
He says *it* takes real courage.

persuasive writing This type of text intends to persuade the reader to a certain standpoint. Powerful language may be used with supporting arguments and evidence. (See pages 36 and 38.)

playscript A playscript is the written down version of a play used by actors. (See page 16.)

plural See **singular**.

pronoun A pronoun is a word that can replace a noun.
For example: *I, me, you, he, him, she, her, we, us, it, they, them, mine, yours, his, hers, ours, theirs, its, myself, herself, himself, themselves.*

poem A poem is a text which creates or recreates experience in a compressed and intense way, using rhythm, or rhyme and language effects to create images and sound effects. (See pages 14, 24 and 40.)

punctuation Punctuation is the term given to those marks used to help a reader, such as full stops (.), question marks (?), commas (,), exclamation marks (!), speech marks (' and '), colons (:) and semi-colons (;).

question mark A question mark (?) is a punctuation mark that is used to end a question sentence.
For example: *What part will you play?*

report This type of text provides information about a subject. (See page 18.)

sentence All sentences begin with a capital letter and most end with a full stop. A sentence must 'make sense', and be complete. There are four types:
1 *Statements* – most sentences are statements that end in a full stop (.).
2 *Questions* – that ask something and end in a question mark (?).
3 *Exclamations* – that exclaim and end in an exclamation mark (!).
4 *Imperatives* – sentences written as commands or instructions, with the verb near the start of the sentence, e.g. Turn the knob.

singular/ plural Singular refers to one thing. Plural refers to more than one thing.
For example:
dog (singular) *sky* (singular) *wolf* (singular) *ditch* (singular)
dogs (plural) *skies* (plural) *wolves* (plural) *ditches* (plural)

speech marks Speech marks (' and ') are punctuation marks that enclose speech, including the relevant sentence punctuation.
For example: *'What is it?' she gasped.*

speech verbs Speech verbs are the verbs used before or after speech to show how the speech has been spoken. The most common is *said*. Others include – *roared, whispered, chanted, muttered,* etc.

story A story is a text type that recounts an invented tale. It is usually used to entertain. Stories usually have a setting, characters and are structured by a plot. (See pages 30, 32 and 34.)

sub-heading A sub-heading comes below a heading and indicates to the reader the contents of smaller units of text.

superlative See **adjective**.

tense A tense is a verb form that shows whether events happen in the past, present or the future. For example:
The Pyramids are on the west bank of the River Nile. (present tense)
They were built as enormous tombs. (past tense)
They will stand for centuries to come. (future tense)
Most verbs change their spelling by adding *ed* to make the past tense, e.g. *walk/walked*. Some have irregular spellings, e.g. *catch/caught*.

title A title is the overall heading given to a text. For example:
The Evacuation

verb A verb shows the action in a sentence and can express a process or state.
1 Verbs are often known as 'doing' or 'happening' words. For example, in the following sentence the word *run* is the verb.
The boys run down the hill.
2 Sometimes several words make up the verb. For instance: *The boys are running*. In this case *running* is the main verb and are is an extra verb that adds to the meaning. It is called an **auxiliary verb**.